Fantastic!
Wow!
And Unreal!

A Book About Interjections
and Conjunctions

To
Totally
Cool!
RONNIE ANN HERMAN

Publishers • GROSSET & DUNLAP • *New York*

Copyright © 1998 by The Ruth Heller Trust. All rights reserved. Published by Grosset & Dunlap, Inc., a member of Penguin Putnam Books for Young Readers, New York. GROSSET & DUNLAP is a trademark of Grosset & Dunlap, Inc. Published simultaneously in Canada. Printed in Singapore.

Library of Congress Cataloging-in-Publication data is available

ISBN 0-448-41862-2   A B C D E F G H I J

Fantastic! Wow! And Unreal!

A Book About Interjections and Conjunctions

Written and illustrated by
RUTH HELLER

INTERJECTIONS
are words
we use
to
declare…

Good
grief!

Out
of
sight!

Holy
cow!

That's
her
hair.

They're capitalized
and punctuated,
and stand alone
when emphatically stated...

My stars!
Sakes alive!
Heavens
above!

The
owl
and
the
pussycat
fell
in
love.

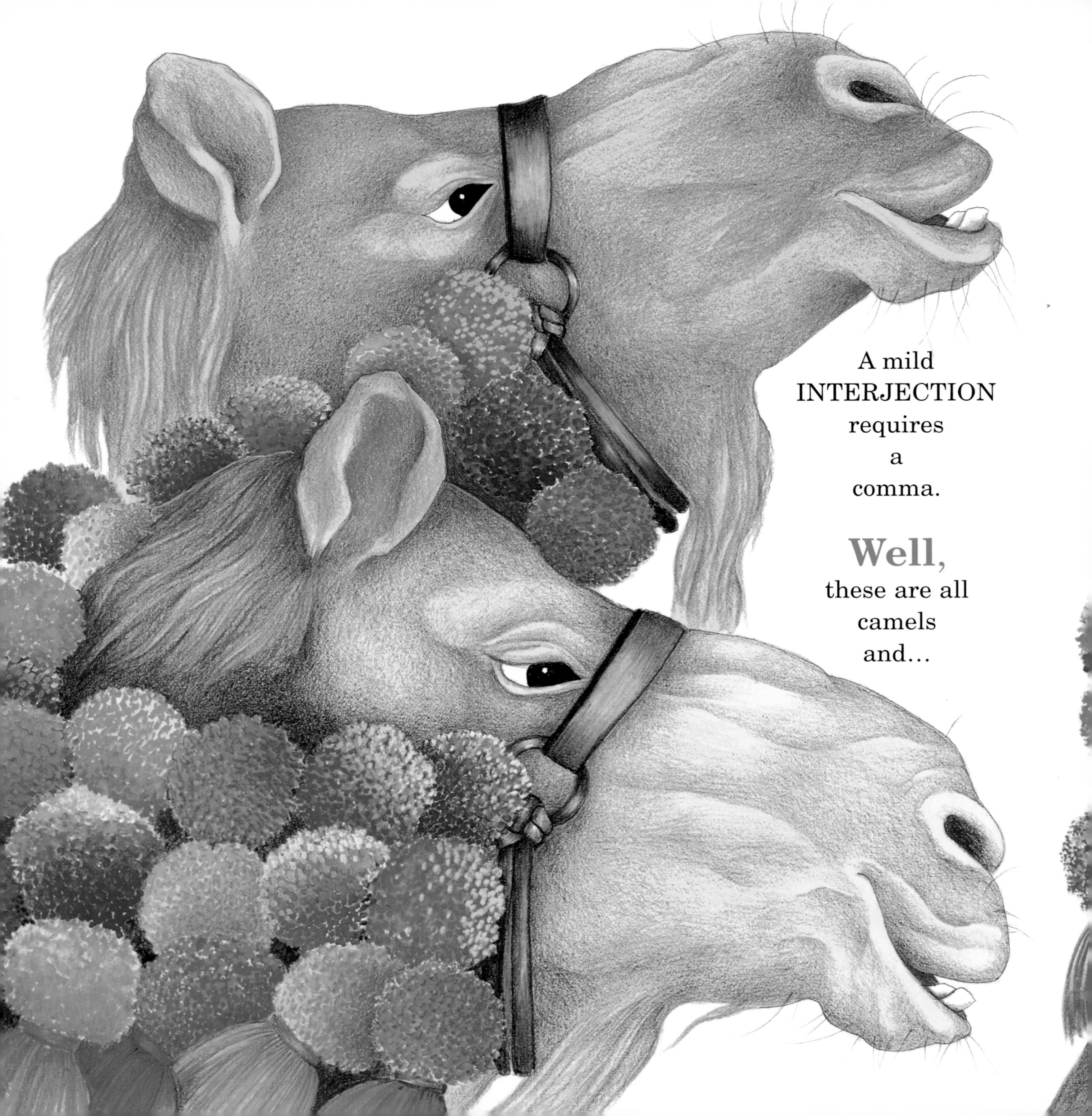

A mild
INTERJECTION
requires
a
comma.

Well,
these are all
camels
and…

...this is a
llama.

Awesome! **Cool!** **Fantastic!** **Wow!**

are all INTERJECTIONS that people say now.

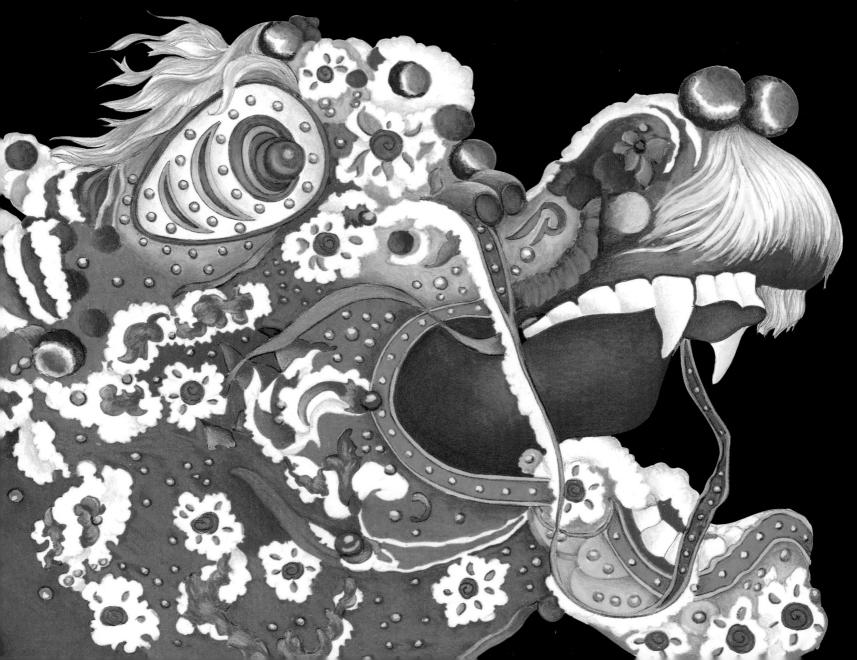

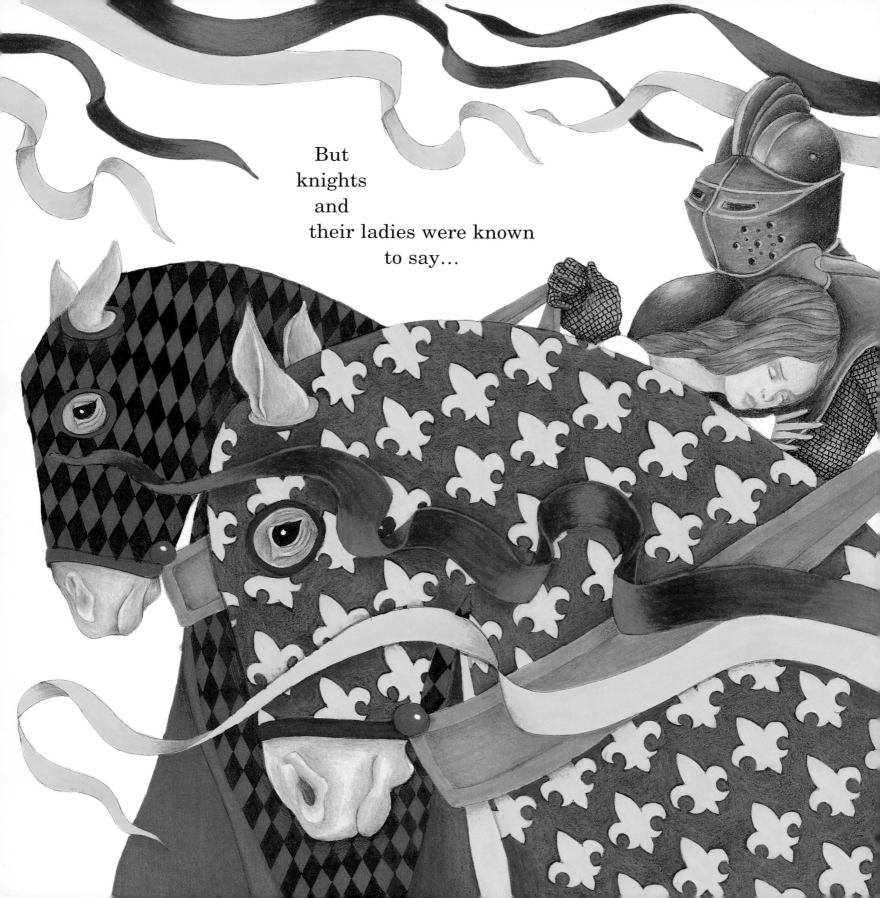

But
knights
and
their ladies were known
to say...

Alas! Alack! when they had a bad day.

INTERJECTIONS change with the times.

As
for
CONJUNCTIONS,
there
is
nothing
new.

•

CONJUNCTIONS
connect.
CONJUNCTIONS
are
glue.

They
join
words
together
and
groups
of
words,
too.

CI LXVII IL

DV XIII MV

Odd…

XV DCLXIX IC

LXXV XCV

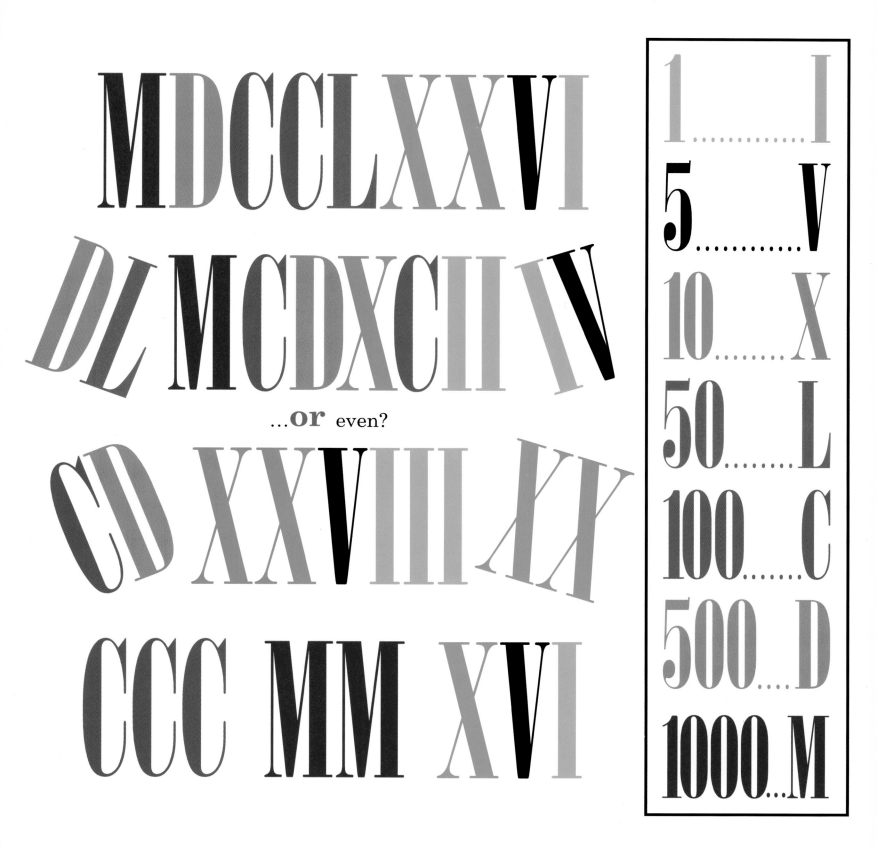

MDCCLXXVI

DL MCDXCII V

...or even?

CD XXVIII XX

CCC MM XVI

1..........I
5..........V
10........X
50........L
100......C
500....D
1000..M

Strange,
yet
true.

These
sea dragons
swim
in the
ocean
blue.

But...

...don't always believe your eyes,
for
no one is tallest,
nor anyone
smallest...

...**so** these people are all the same size.

And
or
yet
but
for
nor
so
are very important CONJUNCTIONS to know...

...and so are **if** and **because** and **although**.

Although this is a...

...wondrous sight, these zebras
do not look quite right,
because...

...they
should
be
black
and
white.

If
ever zebras
looked like these,
they may have had a rare disease.

Some
CONJUNCTIONS
travel
in
pairs.

I'm afraid of
both
tigers
and
bears.

Neither
one
nor

the other one
cares
if
either
their teeth
or

the claws
on their paws
tear
not
only

my nose
but
also

my clothes
and
whatever
they find
underneath.

When adverbs connect,
adverbs are glue.
They behave the same way
CONJUNCTIONS do.

I have a rooster;
furthermore,
I've a hen;
consequently,
I've eggs
that will hatch; and **then**
I'll have a new rooster;
perhaps
a new hen,
since
the very
same thing
often
happens
again.

When
pronouns
connect,
pronouns
are
glue.

They behave the same
way
CONJUNCTIONS
do.

There was
an old woman
who
lived
in
a
shoe.

A
COMPOUND
CONJUNCTION
is
a phrase,
not a word.

As a
matter
of
fact...

…I'm sure
you
have
heard…

…another
old woman
swallowed
a bird.

As a result,
we think her absurd.

Each kind of CONJUNCTION behaves just like glue,
connecting words and groups of words, too.

COORDINATING CONJUNCTIONS

and   or   but   for   nor   yet   so

SUBORDINATING CONJUNCTIONS

**although   if   than   though   unless
because   provided   whereas
whenever**

CORRELATIVE CONJUNCTIONS

**both...and   either...or
neither...nor   whether...or
not only...but also
although...nevertheless**

CONJUNCTIVE ADVERBS

also   consequently   therefore   else
accordingly   hence   furthermore
then   perhaps   as

PRONOUNS used as CONJUNCTIONS

that   who   what   whose   which

COMPOUND CONJUNCTIONS

on the contrary   on the other hand
as a matter of fact   in the meantime
as a result   in addition   in fact
as long as   as soon as
in order to

Congratulations!
Hooray! Hurrah!
Yippee!
Hallelujah!
Whoopee!
and
Aha!